Contents

Contents

Introduction

This is a collection of traditional Welsh recipes, which have been handed down through the centuries. Essentially, the cooking methods and the ingredients used have not changed since pre-medieval times. The principal utensils are a large pot or saucepan for the slow cooking of stews or broth (*cawl*), a griddle, originally a bakestone, and the Dutch oven, in which smaller joints of meat would be cooked.

The recipes themselves rely on good, fresh, usually seasonal ingredients. Adaptability and simplicity are the main features of Welsh cookery, and the experienced cook omits or includes ingredients according to availability. Traditional cookery is still practised today in Wales; each family having its own favourite version of any given recipe.

The simplicity of many of the recipes allows them to be prepared and served when and if there are unexpected visitors or a sudden need to augment the quantity of food for a meal. In Wales, as reflected in its literature, food and drink were an intrinsic part of hospitality, and a host was judged on the quality served at his table. Iolo Goch, a Welsh fourteenth-century poet, praised such hospitality at Sycarth, the court of Owain Glyndŵr: 'There will be … neither want, nor hunger, nor reproach, nor thirst ever at Sycarth.'

Soups

The usual English translation for *cawl* is soup or broth but, as can be seen in the recipes below, *cawl* comes nearer in its consistency to stew. *Cawl*, doubtless, originates from pre-medieval times, when the principal utensil for cooking was a large iron cauldron suspended over an open fire, in which *cawl*, the main meal of the day, was cooked. The meat used in the *cawl* would provide one meal, and the remaining vegetables and stock would provide another. *Cawl* is still popular today in Wales.

LIVER BROTH (*CAWL HASLET*)

450 g (1 lb) pig's liver	*salt and pepper*
450 g (1 lb) peeled potatoes	
450 g (1 lb) onions, sliced	

Cut the liver into small pieces, and prepare the potatoes. Simmer the liver and onions in 1.75 litres (3 pints) of water for 1½ to 2 hours. Add the potatoes, simmer for 30 minutes, season with salt and pepper. Strain and serve very hot.

LAMB BROTH (*CAWL CIG OEN*)

1 kg (2 lb) best end of Welsh
lamb
250 g (8 oz) carrots, halved
1 small swede, sliced
2 large leeks
450 g (1 lb) potatoes, quartered

15 g (½ oz) plain flour
or oatmeal
30 g (1 oz) parsley,
chopped
salt and pepper

Place the meat (whole) into a large saucepan, cover
with cold water, add salt and pepper. Bring gradually to
the boil and skim carefully. Add the carrots, the swede
and the white of the leeks, and simmer gently for 2 to 2½
hours. Add the potatoes and continue to simmer for
another 30 minutes. When the potatoes are almost
cooked, thicken with either oatmeal or flour mixed into
a paste with a little water. Lastly, add the green of the
leeks and the parsley, and simmer for a further 10
minutes. Serve in bowls whilst still hot.

LEEK BROTH (*CAWL CENNIN*)

a piece of salt bacon
450 g (1 lb) carrots, finely diced
450 g (1 lb) potatoes, finely
diced
2 large leeks, sliced
white cabbage, finely shredded

15 ml (1 tbsp) chopped
parsley
30 ml (2 tbsp) oatmeal
(optional)

Place the bacon, carrots and potatoes into enough boiling water to cover them. Boil for 1½ hours, topping up
with water as it boils down. Remove the bacon and add
the leeks together with some finely shredded cabbage.
When these two vegetables are cooked, add the
chopped parsley and serve. Thicken the *cawl* by adding

the oatmeal mixed into a paste with cold water.

TREGARON BROTH (*CAWL TREGARON*)

675 g (1½ lb) bacon	*250 g (8 oz) parsnips*
450 g (1 lb) shin beef	*450 g (1 lb) potatoes*
1 white cabbage	*1 large leek*
250 g (8 oz) carrots	*oatmeal to thicken*
½ small swede	*salt and pepper to taste*

Place all the meat and the vegetables, except the leek, into a large saucepan, ensuring that they are all covered by water. Bring to the boil and leave to simmer until the meat is very tender. Put in the leek 10 minutes before serving, bringing the *cawl* back to full boil.

PEMBROKESHIRE BROTH (*CAWL SIR BENFRO*)

A midday farm meal, which one would begin to prepare at nine o'clock in the morning.

1 kg (2 lb) salted beef	*cabbage, finely shredded*
1 kg (2 lb) bacon	*a little oatmeal*
a few carrots, turnips and	
onions, finely chopped	

Place the meat with 2.25–3.5 litres (4–6 pints) water into a very large saucepan and simmer for 2 hours. Then put the carrots, turnips, onions and cabbage into the saucepan, and continue to simmer for another 30 minutes. Remove the meat and place on a dish, and keep warm. Then add the oatmeal to the *cawl* to thicken it. Serve the broth in bowls, adding finely chopped, cooked leeks, and serve with crusty bread.

The meat is served as a second course with boiled potatoes.

MUTTON BROTH (*CAWL*)

675 g (1½ lb) scrag or best
end of neck of mutton
carrots, diced
potatoes, peeled but left whole
a piece of turnip, diced

50 g (2 oz) pearl barley
parsley, finely chopped
leeks, sliced
salt and pepper

Wash the meat and place it into a large saucepan with 900 ml (1½ pints) cold water. Add the carrots, potatoes, turnip, salt and pepper, and the pearl barley. Bring to the boil and allow to simmer gently for 1½ hours. Then add the parsley and the leeks, washed well in salt water and cut into rings, except the green part, unless the leeks are young. Serve immediately.

WELSH LOBSCOUSE (*LOBSGOWS*)

Lobsgows was eaten generally for dinner on farms or in the quarry districts of north Wales, and it remains a favourite dish today. The amount of the vegetables and meat in this dish is determined by the size of the family.

a piece of salt beef
onions
carrots

swedes
potatoes
salt and pepper to taste

Boil the meat for 5 to 10 minutes, before adding the finely chopped onions, carrots and swedes. Continue to simmer until the meat is almost tender. Add the potatoes, and continue to simmer for 20 minutes. The thickness of the *lobsgows* is determined by the amount of vegetable included.

HARE BROTH (*CAWL YSGYFARNOG*)

This recipe is for an old hare, which should be hung for

at least 1 week before cooking, although some recipes state that the hare should be soaked in water, others say that the jointed hare should only be wiped clean, and never washed.

1 hare	*potatoes*
carrots, finely chopped	*15 ml (1 tbsp) oatmeal*
a little parsley	*a little salt*
a few leeks, sliced	

Skin and dress the hare, which does take some skill, so it may be preferable to ask the butcher to do this. Cut into two joints, and soak overnight in salted water. Put the hare and the carrots into a large saucepan, pour on 7 litres (1½ gallons) cold water and bring to the boil. Add the salt, the parsley and the leek. Mix the oatmeal with a little cold water, and stir it into the broth. Continue to boil until the meat comes free from the bones. Remove the meat from the *cawl*, and then add the potatoes to the broth and boil for some 20 minutes. Eat the broth, the potatoes and the cooked hare together.

QUICK TO MAKE *CAWL*
When there was no time to make *cawl* in the usual way, the meat and the vegetables would be cut up finely, and boiled together quickly.

VEGETABLE BROTH (*CAWL PEN LLETWAD*)
This *cawl* is made with whichever vegetables are available, without the inclusion of any meat in the cooking process.

GOWER OYSTER SOUP (*CAWL WYSTRYS BRO GŴYR*)

50 g (2 oz) butter
40 g (1½ oz) plain flour
2 litres (4 pints) mutton broth, flavoured with onions,
*   ground mace and black pepper*
a quantity of oysters, already bearded

Melt the butter in a pan and blend with the flour. Pour on the mutton broth, and bring to the boil and simmer for 15 minutes until it thickens. Strain and pour over the required quantity of oysters.

Fish and Seafood

COCKLE CAKES (*TEISENNAU COCOS*)

> *2 litres (4 pints) of cockles*
> *30 g (1 oz) oatmeal*
> *hot fat or oil for frying*

Thick batter

> *30 g (1 oz) butter, melted*   *1 egg*
> *100 g (4 oz) plain flour*   *salt and pepper*

Steep the cockles overnight in cold water sprinkled with the oatmeal. Wash well and boil until the shells open. When cool remove the cockles from the shells.

To make the batter add 75 ml (2 to 3 fl oz) water and butter slowly to the sifted flour and seasoning, and beat well. Gradually add the beaten egg, and mix well.

Heat the fat or oil in a deep pan. Dip the cockles one at a time in the batter, and fry, a spoonful at a time, until golden brown, and drain. Serve with fresh lemon slices and thin brown bread and butter.

COCKLE PIE (*PASTAI GOCOS*)

> *shortcrust pastry*   *bunch spring onions or*
> *(following recipe on p. 62)*   *chives, chopped*

1 kg (2 pints) cockles, prepared as above for cockle cakes in one cup of water	250 g (8 oz) bacon, chopped finely pepper

Preheat the oven to 200°C, 400°F, Gas 6. Roll out the pastry thickly, and line the sides of a deep, well greased pie-dish, reserving some to decorate the top of the pie. Put a layer of cockles in the bottom of the dish. Sprinkle with the chives or spring onion, then a layer of the bacon. Repeat these layers until the dish is full. Pour in the liquid in which the cockles were boiled, and sprinkle liberally with ground pepper. Decorate the top with strips of the reserved pastry, making a criss-cross pattern over the pie. Cook in a moderate oven for 30 minutes.

Serve hot with new potatoes, or cold with a salad.

COCKLES (*COCOS*)

The simplest way to cook cockles is to put them in a hot oven (originally a Dutch oven), washing them thoroughly in cold water. When they open, season with pepper or vinegar, and then eat them directly from the shells with bread and butter.

LIMPET PIE (*PASTAI FRENIG*)

bread dough or shortcrust pastry (following recipe on p.62) 1 litre (2 pints) limpets, already cooked 250 g (8 oz) streaky bacon cubed	2 hard-boiled eggs, diced 1 large onion, sliced salt and pepper

11

Preheat the oven to 220°C, 425°F, Gas 7. Line a deep pie dish with either thinly rolled out dough or shortcrust pastry, reserving some for the top of the pie. Fill the lined dish with alternate layers of the limpets, the bacon, the hard-boiled eggs and the onion. Add the seasoning and a little of the limpet liquor. Cover with either the reserved dough or pastry. Bake in a hot oven for 30 minutes, and then more slowly for a further 30 minutes at 190°C, 375°F, Gas 5.

LAVER BREAD (*BARA LAWR*)

Laver is an edible seaweed, which can be bought already processed in Swansea market, and other places along the west coast of Wales; it is also available ready processed and canned. The following recipe shows how to prepare laver bread if fresh seaweed is available.

> seaweed   bacon fat
> fine oatmeal

Wash the seaweed well to remove the sand. Boil for several hours until it is tender. Mix with fine oatmeal, and form into small cakes. Fry, usually with bacon fat, and serve with bacon for breakfast.

Various uses for laver bread:
Eat laver bread cold with vinegar, as is the custom in Cornwall.

Mix laver bread with fine oatmeal, then coat with oatmeal and fry in bacon fat.

Fry thick slices of bread, spread with hot laver bread, in bacon fat, topped with chopped bacon or ham, salt and pepper.

Heat a tablespoon of butter in a pan, put in laver

bread with a squeeze of lemon juice and spread on hot, buttered toast.

FRESHWATER FISH

The usual way of cooking fish caught fresh from the river was fried. The cleaned fish was cooked in bacon fat or butter, and eaten either for dinner or supper.

SALMON AND ONIONS (*EOG A WINWNS*)

a piece of salmon	*bacon fat*
onions, finely chopped	*salt*

Clean the fish, and wash it thoroughly. Place the fish in salted water, and boil it for several minutes. Lift the fish from the water, and pull the skin and the bones away. Flake the fish and fry it with the onions in bacon fat.

BAKED TROUT AND BACON (BRYTHYLL A CHIG MOCH)

slices of fatty bacon	*chopped parsley*
trout	*salt and pepper*

Preheat the oven to 180°C, 350°F, Gas 4. Grease and line a shallow pie dish with thin slices of fatty bacon. Split and clean the trout and place them on the bacon. Sprinkle with chopped parsley, salt and pepper. Cover and bake for approximately 20 minutes.

SUPPER HERRINGS (*SWPER 'SCADAN*)

450 g (1 lb) medium-sized	*1 large cooking apple*
herrings	*boiling water*
5 ml (1 tsp) mustard	*5 ml (1 tsp) sage*

        675 g (1½ lb) potatoes   15 g (½ oz) butter
        1 large onion   salt and pepper

Preheat the oven to 190°C, 375°F, Gas 5. Clean herrings, bone and divide into fillets. Spread the prepared fillets with the mustard, and sprinkle with the salt and pepper, and roll up. Peel and slice the potatoes and the onion. Peel and core the apple. Line the bottom of a greased pie-dish with half of the potatoes, then cover with half of the apple, the onion and, then, the rolled herrings. Sprinkle with the sage. Cover with the remaining apple and potatoes and seasoning, and half-fill the dish with boiling water. Cover the top with little knobs of butter, cover, and bake in a moderate oven for 30 minutes. Remove the cover and continue to cook in the oven for another 30 minutes.

TEIFI SALMON IN SAUCE (*EOG TEIFI MEWN SAWS*)

        1 fresh salmon   15 ml (1 tbsp) ketchup
        450 ml (¾ pint) melted butter   1 anchovy fillet
        1 glass port   salt

Preheat the oven to 190°C, 375°F, Gas 5. Wash the salmon in salted water, dry carefully and cut into slices. In a pan, set over a low heat, blend together the melted butter, the port, the ketchup and the anchovy. Pour this sauce over the salmon, and put in a covered dish in a fairly hot oven, and bake for about ¾ hour.

SALMON TROUT (*SEWIN or GWYNIEDYN*)

Salmon trout is still caught today in the rivers Teifi and Twyi, by the same fishing techniques that were used over 2,000 years ago. Salmon trout should be simply

14

cooked, by poaching, and served cold, so that its full flavour can be appreciated. Salmon can be cooked and served in the same way.

a sprig or two of fennel   *a little salt*
1 kg (2 lb) salmon trout

Bring some salted water, with the fennel added, to the boil in a large saucepan. Lower the fish carefully into the water, and simmer. Allow 15 minutes to each 450 grams (1 lb) of fish. Lift the fish from the water, and leave it to drain completely before cutting it into slices.

Serve warm with parsley sauce, or cold, either with a coating of fresh cream, or with bread and butter and salad.

STUFFED SALMON (*SEWIN*)
Fill the fish with a stuffing made from parsley and thyme, and then roast in bacon fat.

15

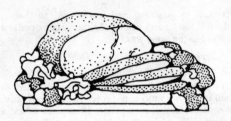

Meat

KATT PIE

A very old recipe. Katt Pie was traditionally made on Templeton Fair Day (12 November), for at least 200 years, and is very similar to the original recipe for mince pies, eaten at Christmas.

100 g (4 oz) suet	*100 g (4 oz) brown sugar*
450 g (1 lb) flour	*100 g (4 oz) currants*
100 g (4 oz) minced mutton	*salt and pepper*

Preheat the oven to 220°C, 425°F, Gas 7. Make hot water crust pastry by boiling the suet in water. Add to the flour with a good pinch of salt, and mix well with a wooden spoon. When cool, roll out and make into individual pies about 10 cm (4 in) in diameter. Arrange the filling in the following layers: mutton, currants and sugar, salt and pepper. Top with a round of thin pastry. Bake in a hot oven for 20 to 30 minutes.

Eat while still hot.

ROOK PIE (*PASTAI BRAIN BACH*)

It was traditional in Wales (and in other country areas of Great Britain) for farmers to have a rook shoot in May, when many young rooks were shot. The following recipe demonstrates how nothing went to waste in the farming areas of Wales. The pie can be made with any other game bird or poultry with good results.

Preheat the oven to 200°C, 400°F, Gas 6. Only the breasts and a little of the upper legs, which must be skinned, are used, for the backbone has a bitter taste. The meat is seasoned and put in a pie dish lined with shortcrust pastry. To the meat is added finely chopped bacon, chives and thyme, and a little stock added. The pie is covered with pastry and baked in a moderate oven.

WELSH CHICKEN (*CIG CYW IÂR CYMREIG*)

1 or 2 chickens, depending on weight	30 g (1 oz) plain flour
100 g (4 oz) bacon	1 small cabbage, sliced
2 large leeks, sliced	bunch of mixed herbs
100 g (4 oz) carrots, sliced	300 ml (½ pint) stock
30 g (1 oz) butter	dripping or butter
	salt and pepper

Boiling chicken should ideally be used, but young chicken can be used instead, adjusting the cooking time accordingly. Dice the bacon and carrots. Place them in a saucepan with the butter and fry for a few minutes, then stir in the flour until it thickens and browns. Place the chickens and the cabbage into the casserole, resting them on the cooked vegetables and thickened sauce. Add the herbs and leeks and sprinkle on the salt and pepper. Add the stock, put some small knobs of dripping (or butter) on the chicken, cover

17

and simmer for 2 to 3 hours (making sure that the chicken has at least 20 mins per lb cooking time). On serving make a bed of the cabbage on a dish, and place the cooked chicken on it. Garnish with the carrots and pour the gravy over the cabbage. This recipe can also be cooked successfully in a large, lidded saucepan on the hob.

PEMBROKESHIRE FAGGOTS (*FFAGOTS SIR BENFRO*)

This was a popular dish prepared after pig killing in Pembrokeshire some 100 years ago.

450 g (1 lb) pig's liver	10 ml (2 tsp) chopped
2 large onions	sage
100 g (4 oz) fresh breadcrumbs	10 ml (2 tsp) salt
75 g (3 oz) suet	2.5 ml (½ tsp) pepper

Mince the raw liver and the onions and place into a mixing bowl. Mix thoroughly with the breadcrumbs, the suet, the sage and the salt and pepper. Form the mixture into small balls. Place into a greased oven tin and bake in a moderate oven for approximately 30 minutes. Pour boiling water into the tin to form the gravy.

WELSH LAMB PIE (*PASTAI GIG OEN*)

This is an old recipe.

675 g (1½ lb) neck of Welsh	salt and pepper
lamb	shortcrust pastry
1 small bunch young carrots	(following recipe on p.62)
10 ml (2 tsp) chopped	milk
parsley	

For the gravy:

the lamb bones

1 onion

salt and pepper

Preheat the oven to 200°C, 400°F, Gas 6. Bone the meat and cut it into small pieces. Clean and finely slice the carrots into rounds, and place a layer of them on the bottom of a greased dish, then the meat, parsley and salt and pepper. Repeat the layers until all the ingredients are used. Cover with water, about 2 inches from the top of the dish. Cover with the prepared pastry and brush liberally with milk. Bake for 20 minutes, then lower the temperature to 180°C, 350°F, Gas 4 for 1 hour 40 minutes.

Boil the bones, the onion and the salt and pepper in sufficient water for 1½ hours, and when the pie is ready, strain and pour into the pie. This pie can be served hot or cold.

RABBIT PIE (*PASTAI GWINGEN*)

1 rabbit, dressed and jointed

250 g (8 oz) beef steak

100 g (4 oz) cooked ham

stock

10 ml (2 tsp) parsley, chopped

ground nutmeg

salt and pepper

shortcrust pastry

(following recipe on

p. 62)

Soak the cleaned rabbit in salt water for at least 1½ hours, then place in a pie dish together with the steak and the ham, cut into small pieces. Sprinkle with parsley, and salt, pepper and nutmeg, add enough stock to cover all the ingredients. Place the pastry on top. Bake slowly for approximately 1½ hours.

19

Alternately cook the rabbit as above, without covering it with pastry, but in a covered casserole. When cooked cover with pastry and cook in a hot oven (200°C, 400°F, Gas 6) for 20 minutes.

MASHED POTATO AND LIVER (*STWNS RWDAN AC IAU*)

This is a popular dish in north Wales. It is customary in Wales to mash potatoes (*stwnsio*) with a variety of vegetables. One dish made with mashed potatoes is still prepared today: make a *stwns* and serve with buttermilk poured over it.

450 g (1 lb) liver	1 large onion, sliced
Flour, seasoned with salt and pepper	potatoes
	swede

Prepare the liver by cutting it into slices and fry until it is dark brown. Roll the cooked liver in the flour. Fry the onions and roll them also in the seasoned flour. Put the liver and the onions into a large saucepan or into a casserole, cover with water, and simmer very slowly for 2 to 3 hours.

Boil the potatoes and swede. Serve the liver with the potatoes and the swede well mashed together to make the *stwns*.

Alternatives
stwns pys – potatoes and peas mashed together.
stwns ffa – potatoes and broad beans mashed together.

MISER'S FEAST (*FFEST/GWLEDD Y CYBYDD*)

This dish was popular in Carmarthenshire some 150 years ago, when it was cooked in a saucepan.

peeled potatoes	*bacon or a piece of ham*
sliced onion	*salt*

Cover the bottom of a saucepan or casserole with the potatoes and the onion, and season with a little salt. Cover with water and bring to the boil. When the water is boiling, place on top of the vegetables slices of bacon or a piece of ham. Cover with a lid and simmer until the potatoes are cooked, and most of the water has been absorbed.

Eat the potatoes, mashed with some of the liquid, and save the bacon or ham to be eaten the next day with plain boiled potatoes.

MEAT AND POTATO PIE

This pie was made at the end of the reaping season in some agricultural areas of Wales.

1 kg (2 lb) potatoes	*1 rasher bacon, chopped*
a knob of butter	*250 g (8 oz) minced*
15 ml (1 tbsp) of flour	*cooked meat*
1 onion, chopped	*salt and pepper*

Preheat the oven to 200°C, 400°F, Gas 6. Boil the potatoes, then mash, adding a knob of butter and the flour. Fry the chopped onion and bacon, then add to the mashed potatoes with the minced meat. Season, and mix all together and then turn into a greased pie-dish. Bake in a moderate oven for about 20 minutes until the top is golden brown.

ROAST BEEF, POTATOES AND ONIONS

    45 ml (3 tbsp) beef dripping   *1 large onion*
    a joint of roasting beef   *15 ml (1 tbsp) flour*
    1 kg (2 lb) potatoes   *salt and pepper*

Preheat the oven to 190°C, 375°F, Gas 5. Spread the
dripping over the beef, basting occasionally. Peel and
halve the potatoes, and peel and thinly slice the onion.
Place the potatoes round the meat, and put the sliced
onions on top of them. Sprinkle the vegetables with the
flour, seasoned with salt and pepper. Pour enough water
into the roasting tin for it to reach half-way round the
potatoes. Continue to cook in the oven, until the potatoes are golden brown.

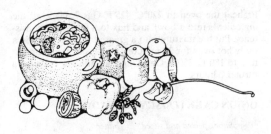

Vegetables

POTATO CAKES (*TEISENNAU TATWS*)

600 ml (1 pint) milk
30 g (1 oz) yeast
40 g (1½ oz) butter

250 g (8 oz) boiled potatoes
350 g (12 oz) flour
pinch of salt

Warm the milk, and dissolve in it the yeast and the butter, then stir into the potatoes and mix well. Knead this liquid into the flour. Place in a warm place to prove for 1 hour. Shape into small cakes, and bake in a moderate oven, until golden brown.

POTATO CAKE (*TEISEN DATWS*)

This cake can be eaten hot or cold, sliced and spread with butter.

450 g (1 lb) cold boiled
potatoes
45 ml (3 tbsp) plain flour
5 ml (1 tsp) baking powder

30 ml (2 tbsp) brown sugar
1.5 ml (¼ tsp) cinnamon
milk to mix

23

Preheat the oven to 220°C, 425°F, Gas 7. Place all the ingredients into a bowl, and mix to a fairly stiff consistency. Put the mixture into a greased tin, and place in a fairly hot oven for 20 minutes, then lower the temperature to 180°C, 350°F, Gas 4, and continue to bake for a further 2 hours.

ONION CAKE (*TEISEN NIONED*)

> potatoes, peeled and sliced butter
> onions, finely chopped   salt and pepper

Preheat the oven to 190°C, 375°F, Gas 5. Place a layer of sliced potatoes on the bottom of a well-buttered cake tin. Sprinkle a layer of chopped onions on the potatoes, season with salt and pepper, and cover with small knobs of butter. Repeat these layers until the tin is full, the final layer being a layer of potato, on which a layer of butter is spread. Cover with a lid or a plate and cook for 1 hour in a moderate oven.

Eat this cake either hot or cold with cooked meat.

POTATO AND 'CHEESE' TARTLETS

> shortcrust pastry (following 100 g (4 oz) currants
> recipe on p. 62)   100 g (4 oz) sugar
> 250 g (8 oz) mashed potatoes 100 g (4 oz) butter

Preheat the oven to 200°C, 400°F, Gas 6. Line greased patty tins with the pastry. Mix all the other ingredients thoroughly together, and fill the pastry-lined tins with the mixture. Bake in an oven until golden brown.

LEEK PASTY (*PASTAI GENNIN*)

350 g (12 oz) plain flour
175 g (6 oz) lard
5 ml (1 tsp) baking powder
a pinch of salt

2 to 3 handfuls of leeks
a few strips of fat bacon
salt and pepper

Preheat the oven to 200°C, 400°F, Gas 6. Rub together the flour, baking powder, salt and lard. Mix into a paste with cold water. Cut the paste in two, roll out thinly enough to cover a large dinner plate. Slice the leeks finely, and cover one layer of the pastry, placing the strips of bacon on top of the leeks. Season with salt and pepper to taste, adding a scant amount of cold water. Cover with the other layer of prepared pastry, and cook in a hot oven until golden brown.

MARROW PIE (1) (*PASTAI FARO*)

Dishes made with vegetable marrow were very popular in medieval Wales.

1 medium-sized vegetable
    marrow
shortcrust pastry (following
    recipe on p. 62)

250 g (8 oz) sugar
250 g (8 oz) currants
1.5 ml (¼ tsp) nutmeg
15 ml (1 tbsp) vinegar

Preheat the oven to 190°C, 375°F, Gas 5. Peel the marrow, remove the centre, and cut the remainder into cubes. Grease and line a pie dish with half the shortcrust pastry. Then put a layer of the cubed marrow into it, a layer of the sugar, a layer of the currants, and a sprinkling of nutmeg. Continue these layers until the pie dish is full. Add the vinegar. Cover with the remaining pastry, and bake in a moderately hot oven until the marrow is tender.

Serve hot or cold.

MARROW PIE (2) (*PASTAI FARO*)

shortcrust pastry (following recipe on p. 62)	100 g (4 oz) sugar
1 medium-sized vegetable marrow	a pinch of ground ginger
a few crab apples	1 egg
a few cloves	salt
	a little milk

Preheat the oven to 200°C, 400°F, Gas 6. Line a fairly large, greased pie dish with half the shortcrust pastry. Peel and slice the marrow and crab apples. Place the marrow and crab apples in layers in the pie dish, sprinkling each layer with cloves, sugar, salt and a little water. The final layer should be a layer of crab apple and a little ginger. Cover the pie with the remaining pastry, and decorate it with leaves made from the pastry trimmings. Brush the top with the beaten egg, and bake in a moderate oven for 1 hour.

GLAMORGAN SAUSAGES (*SELSIG MORGANNWG*)

a little onion, finely chopped	150 g fresh bread- crumbs
a pinch of dried mixed herbs	
a pinch of dried mustard	pork dripping or bacon fat
150 g (5 oz) grated cheese	salt and pepper
1 egg, separated	
flour	

Mix together the onion, herbs, mustard and cheese, and

season. Bind together with the egg yolk. Divide the mixture into small sausages, and roll in flour. Dip each sausage in the egg white, then roll in the breadcrumbs. Fry in pork dripping or bacon fat.

Serve hot with mashed potatoes or chips.

Griddle Cakes and Pancakes

WELSH CAKES (1) *(PICE/PICAU AR Y MAEN)*
These cakes were originally cooked on a bakestone.

*350 g (12 oz) butter or 250 g
(8 oz) butter mixed with
100 g (4 oz) lard
450 g (1 lb) plain flour
5 ml (1 tsp) baking powder*

*100 g (4 oz) currants
sufficient milk to make
a soft dough (ideally
buttermilk)*

Rub the butter (or butter and lard) into the flour. Add the dry ingredients, then gradually mix in the milk to make a soft dough. Roll out, cut into rounds. Bake the cakes on both sides on a greased griddle, or in a heavy-based frying-pan, until golden brown.

Sprinkle with caster sugar, if desired.

WELSH CAKES (2) (*PICE/PICAU AR Y MAEN*)

50 g (2 oz) butter or margarine	50 g (2 oz) currants
50 g (2 oz) lard	1.5 ml (¼ tsp) mixed spice
250 g (8 oz) plain flour	1 egg, beaten
2.5 ml (½ tsp) baking powder	a little milk
75 g (3 oz) sugar	pinch of salt

Rub the butter and the lard into the flour. Add the dry ingredients, then the egg and milk. Mix, and form into a firm paste. Roll out, and cut into rounds and bake on a greased griddle, or in a heavy-based frying-pan.

GRIDDLE CAKE (1) (*TEISEN LAP*)

A griddle cake, made to a fairly wet mixture.

100 g (4 oz) fat	7.5 ml (1½ tsp) bicarbonate of soda
450 g (1 lb) plain flour	
100 g (4 oz) brown sugar	300 ml (½ pint) buttermilk or sour milk
100 g (4 oz) mixed dried fruit	
2.5 ml (½ tsp) mixed spice	1 egg

Rub the fat into the flour, add the sugar, the fruit and the spice. Mix well. Dissolve the bicarbonate of soda in the buttermilk or sour milk mixing in the beaten egg. Add the mixture to the dry ingredients and beat until a very soft dough is formed. Divide in two, and roll out into rounds, approximately 2.5 cm (1 in) in thickness. Bake on a greased griddle or in a heavy-based frying-pan for about 15 minutes. When golden brown on one side, turn over.

See page 50 for an oven-baked version for *teisen lap*.

GRIDDLE CAKE (2) (*TEISEN GRI*)

Teisen gri is a griddle cake that is not sweetened with sugar. It was usually made when bread was scarce.

100 g (4 oz) butter	*5 ml (1 tsp) baking powder*
100 g (4 oz) lard	*5 ml (1 tsp) salt*
450 g (1 lb) plain flour	*1 egg*
50 g (2 oz) dried fruit	*a little milk*

GRIDDLE CAKE (3) (*TEISEN GRI*)

100 g (4 oz) butter and lard	*2.5 ml (¼ tsp) baking powder*
450 g (1 lb) plain flour	*a good pinch of salt*
1 egg	*a little milk*
50 g (2 oz) currants	

The same method is used for the above two recipes.

Rub the fat into the flour, add the fruit, baking powder and salt, then mix in the beaten egg and the milk. Form into a stiff paste, roll out thinly, cut into rounds. Bake on a greased, floured griddle, or in a heavy-based frying-pan. Serve hot, spread with butter. Do not split the cakes.

GRIDDLE CAKE (4) (*TEISEN GRI*)

A version of *teisen gri* in which sugar is included.

30 g or 50 g (1 or 2 oz) butter	*50 g (2 oz) dried fruit*
250 g (8 oz) flour	*a little milk as necessary*
30 g or 50 g (1 or 2 oz) sugar	*a pinch of bicarbonate of soda*
2 beaten eggs	*a pinch of baking powder*

Rub the butter into the flour. Add the remaining ingredients and beat to make a thick batter. Place the batter in spoonfuls on a griddle and cook on both sides.

Eat hot, split and buttered.

ANGLESEY GRIDDLE CAKE (*SLAPAN SIR FÔN*)

250 g (8 oz) fat	*5 ml (1 tsp) baking powder*
450 g (1 lb) plain flour	*250 g (8 oz) caster sugar*
100 g (4 oz) currants	*a little milk*
3 beaten eggs	*pinch of salt*

Rub the fat into the flour. Add the salt, currants and eggs. Beat all well. Then stir in the baking powder, sugar and a little milk if necessary. Grease a griddle or a heavy frying-pan with lard. Heat until quite hot, and put the mixture on in spoonfuls. Bake on both sides, and serve hot.

OATMEAL CAKES (*BARA CEIRCH*)

Oatcakes were the alternative to bread for the people who inhabited the mountainous areas of Wales in the eighteenth century.

7.5 ml (½ tbsp) bacon fat	*hot water*
or butter	*a pinch of salt*
60 ml (4 tbsp) oatmeal	

Put 45 ml (3 tbsp) hot water and the fat into a bowl and then drop the oatmeal and salt between the fingers into it until a soft dough is formed. Place on a board which has been spread with oatmeal, press down with the hand, and roll it over evenly to the thickness desired.

Press round the edge until it is even. Roll again. Cut into rounds, either large or small. Bake on a moderately hot griddle or in a thick frying-pan for about 10 minutes. Allow to dry until crisp. Originally it was the custom to allow the oatcakes to harden on a type of shovel (*diogyn*), literally a 'sluggard', before the oven fire.

OATMEAL PANCAKES (1) (*CREMPOGAU CEIRCH*)

250 g (8 oz) oatmeal	a little milk
450 g (1 lb) plain flour	1 egg
10 ml (2 tsp) baking powder	5 ml (1 tsp) salt
30 g (1 oz) yeast	

Soak the oatmeal in water overnight. Place the flour, salt and the baking powder in a bowl and add the yeast mixed with a little milk. Add the egg, well beaten, and the soaked oatmeal. It is important not to add too much of the oatmeal mixture; the mixture should drop off a spoon, but not be too runny.

Cook as pancakes and spread with butter. Sugar can be sprinkled on the pancakes when cooked if you wish. Oatmeal pancakes can be reheated and served with bacon.

OATMEAL PANCAKES (2) (*CREMPOGAU CEIRCH*)

450 g (1 lb) plain flour	15 g (½ oz) yeast, mixed
175 g (6 oz) fine oatmeal	with warm milk and
milk	a little sugar

Blend the flour and oatmeal, add the yeast with sufficient milk to make a thin batter. Cook as pancakes. Eat hot, spread with butter.

LARGE PANCAKE WITH HAM (*PANCOSEN FAWR*)

> *175 g (6 oz) self-raising flour*
> *50 g to 75 g (2 oz to 3 oz) sugar*
> *1.5 ml (¼ tsp) bicarbonate of soda*
>
> *1 egg*
> *milk to mix*
> *4 slices home-cured ham*

Mix the dry ingredients together. Beat the egg, and add to the dry ingredients, adding milk to form a fairly thick batter. In a large frying-pan cook the ham, then keep it warm in a heated dish until required. Pour the batter into the hot fat reserved from the fried ham, and cook both sides until the pancake is golden brown. Cut the pancake into four equal portions, and serve hot.

PANCAKE BATTER (*PONCO*)

> *250 g (8 oz) plain flour*
> *2.5 ml (½ tsp) baking powder*
>
> *milk to mix*
> *a pinch of salt*

Make a batter with the above ingredients, beating the batter well. After frying bacon or ham, leave the residue fat in the pan, and pour the batter into it. Fry until the pancake is golden brown on both sides.

This pancake can be eaten either with bacon and tomatoes, or with a hot meal of meat and vegetables.

PANCAKE OMELETTE (*CREMPOG LAS*)

> *250 g (8 oz) plain flour*
> *5 ml (1 tsp) parsley, chopped*
> *5 ml (1 tsp) shallot, chopped*
>
> *2 eggs*
> *a little milk to mix*
> *salt and pepper*

Blend the flour together with the seasoning, the parsley and the shallot. Beat the eggs, and add to the flour with sufficient milk to make a very thick batter. Beat the batter really well. Fry in a well-greased frying-pan, until golden brown on both sides.

Spread with butter and eat hot.

BUTTERMILK CAKES

45 ml (3 tbsp) strong white flour
7.5ml (1½ tbsp) bicarbonate of soda

600 ml (1 pint) butter-milk
a pinch of salt

Put the flour and salt into a basin. Put the bicarbonate of soda into the buttermilk, and then gradually add to the flour, whilst beating well until the batter is quite smooth. Fry in a frying-pan, as one would for pancakes.

Serve spread with plenty of butter.

SNOW PANCAKES (*CRAMOTH EIRA*)

Snow was used to make these pancakes when eggs were not available in the winter months.

600 ml (1 pint) fresh, clean snow
250 g (8 oz) plain flour

milk
sugar

Mix the snow and flour until the batter is smooth and free of lumps. Add sufficient milk to make a good, stiff batter, add sugar according to taste, and fry as for pancakes.

Serve with slices of lemon.

SOUR MILK PANCAKES (*PANCWS LLAETH SUR*)

75 g (3 oz) butter
250 g (8 oz) self-raising flour
a pinch of ground nutmeg
2 eggs
5 ml (1 tsp) bicarbonate of
  soda

300 ml (½ pint) sour
  milk
1.5 ml (¼ tsp) salt
75 g (3 oz) sugar

Rub the butter into the flour. Add the salt, the sugar and the nutmeg. Mix well together. Beat the eggs, and add to the flour. Dissolve the bicarbonate of soda in the sour milk, and stir until it becomes effervescent, and then add to the mixture. Drop from a dessertspoon on to a hot, well-greased griddle or thick-based frying-pan, and bake until light brown on both sides.

Serve hot, well buttered and piled high.

PIKELETS (*PICE' R PREGETHWR*)

75 g (3 oz) butter
100 g (4 oz) flour
2 eggs

300 ml (½ pint) butter-
  milk or milk

Rub the butter into the flour, beat the eggs with the buttermilk or milk and mix into a batter. Beat in well with a wooden spoon. Ideally the batter should be left to stand overnight. Bake on a well-greased griddle or a heavy-based frying-pan, until both sides are golden brown.

Serve hot and well buttered.

RICE CAKES (*TEISEN REIS*)

250 g (8 oz) boiled rice
15 ml (1 tbsp) melted butter

250 g (8 oz) flour
150 ml (¼ pint) milk

1 egg   5 ml (1 tsp) salt
10 ml (2 tsp) baking powder

Mix the rice, the butter, the salt and the egg, well beaten, together. Sieve together the baking powder and the flour, and mix in the milk, adding more if necessary, and stir well. Drop large tablespoonfuls of the mixture on to a hot greased griddle or thick frying-pan. Cook the cakes for approximately 4 minutes on each side.

Serve hot, with golden syrup if desired.

WELSH CRUMPETS (*CRAMPOETHAU*)

450 g (1 lb) flour   1 beaten egg
2.5 ml (½ tsp) baking powder   600 ml (1 pint) milk
50 g to 75 g (2 oz to 3 oz)   a little cream (optional)
   brown sugar

Place the dry ingredients into a large bowl. Mix the egg with the milk, and if possible with a little cream. Add the liquid gradually to the flour, and mix gradually to form a smooth batter. Cook on a griddle or thick frying-pan, as for pancakes.

Butter and sprinkle liberally with caster sugar.

Cakes and Puddings

SPECKLED BREAD (1) (*BARA BRITH*)

450 g (1 lb) mixed dried fruit
300 ml (½ pint) warm black
   tea
250 g (8 oz) brown sugar, or
   white granulated sugar

10 ml (2 level tsp)
   mixed spice
450 g (1 lb) self-raising
   flour
1 egg

Soak the fruit with the tea, strained, and the sugar in a
large bowl, and leave overnight. The following day,
preheat the oven to 170°C, 325°F, Gas 3. Mix the remaining ingredients into the prepared fruit mixture, and beat
well. Pour the mixture into a loaf tin, which has been well
greased or lined with buttered paper. Bake for 1½ hours.
   Serve sliced and spread with butter.

SPECKLED BREAD (2) (*BARA BRITH*)
A very old recipe.

250 g (8 oz) lard
900 g (2 lb) plain flour

5 ml (1 good tsp)
   baking powder

450 g (1 lb) granulated sugar	5 ml (1 tsp) cream of
250 g (8 oz) raisins	tartar
250 g (8 oz) currants	buttermilk to mix
100 g (4 oz) lemon peel, grated	

Preheat the oven to 170ºC, 325ºF, Gas 3. Rub the lard into the flour, add the sugar, raisins, currants, lemon peel, baking powder and cream of tartar. Mix with enough buttermilk until the whole is a light, soft dough. Bake in two well-greased loaf tins in a warm oven for 1½ hours.

HONEY CAKES (*TEISENNAU MÊL*)

250 g (8 oz) plain flour	100 g (4 oz) brown
5 ml (1 tsp) cinnamon	sugar
2.5 ml (½ tsp) bicarbonate	1 egg, separated
of soda	100 g (4 oz) honey
100 g (4 oz) butter	a little milk to mix

Preheat the oven to 200ºC, 400ºF, Gas 6. Sieve the flour, cinnamon and bicarbonate together. Cream the butter and the sugar. Beat the egg yolk into the creamed sugar and butter, then gradually add the honey. Stir in the sifted ingredients with a little milk, as required, and mix all together lightly. Whisk the egg white until stiff, and fold gently into the mixture. Half-fill prepared bun tins with the mixture, dredging the top of each with caster sugar. Bake in a hot oven for 20 minutes. When ready sprinkle each cake with a little more of the caster sugar.

BERFFRO CAKES

Berffro is the local name for Aberffraw, Anglesey, from where these cakes originate. It is customary to mark each round with a scallop shell, before baking.

> 250 g (8 oz) plain flour   100 g (4 oz) butter
> 50 g (2 oz) sugar

Preheat the oven to 170°C, 325°F, Gas 3. Mix the flour and the sugar thoroughly together. Either rub the butter into the mixture, or melt the butter and mix it well into the mixture. Roll out the dough thinly, and cut into rounds with a cutter. Bake on a greased baking tin in a moderate oven.

SEED CAKE (*CACEN HADAU*)

This recipe is some 250 years old. *Let the fierceness of the oven be over before you set in the cake for fear of scorching it.*

> 900 g (2 lb) of caster sugar   20 ml (4 tsp) orange flower
> 900 g (2 lb) butter   water
> 10 eggs   350 g (12 oz) caraway seeds
> 1.1 kg (2½ lb) flour   250 g (8 oz) candied peel

Preheat the oven to 170°C, 325°F, Gas 3. Cream together the sugar and the butter. Add the eggs one at a time alternately with the flour, then add the orange flower water, the caraway seeds, and the candied peel. Put the mixture in greased tins, when the oven is ready. Bake for 1 hour then turn down to 150°C, 300°F, Gas 2 for ½ hour and finally 140°C, 275°F, Gas 1 for ½ hour until cooked.

SEED LOAF (*TORTH HADAU*)

> 450 g (1 lb) self-raising flour   65 g (2½ oz) butter
> 5 ml (1 tsp) salt   30 g (1 oz) sugar

7.5 ml (½ tbsp) caraway seeds
1 egg beaten with 150 ml
(¼ pint) of milk, or milk
and water

Preheat the oven to 190°C, 375°F, Gas 5. Sieve the flour and the salt into a basin. Rub in the butter and then add the other dry ingredients. Mix into a soft dough with the egg and milk. Place in a greased bread tin. Bake for 1 hour in a moderate oven.

SHEARING CAKE (*CACEN GNEIFI*)

This cake would be prepared for shearing time.

100 g (4 oz) butter	a little grated nutmeg
250 g (8 oz) plain flour	175 g (6 oz) moist
rind of half a lemon	sugar
5 ml (1 tsp) baking powder	150 ml (¼ pint) milk
10 ml (2 tsp) caraway seeds	1 beaten egg

Preheat the oven to 200°C, 400°F, Gas 6. Rub the butter into the flour. Mix all the dry ingredients together and stir in the milk and the egg. Bake in a lined, greased cake tin, in a moderate oven for 1 hour.

OVERNIGHT CAKE (*TEISEN DROS NOS*)

100 g (4 oz) fat	50 g (2 oz) mixed dry
250 g (8 oz) plain flour	fruit
75 g to 100 g (3 oz to	milk
4 oz) sugar	15 ml (1 tbsp) vinegar
5 ml (1 tsp) cinnamon	2.5 ml (½ tsp) bicar-
5 ml (1 tsp) ginger	bonate of soda

Rub the fat into the flour and add the rest of the dry

ingredients except the bicarbonate of soda. Mix with some milk into a fairly soft consistency. Mix the vinegar quickly with the bicarbonate of soda, and thoroughly stir into the mixture. Leave this batter mixture overnight. Bake the next day in a lined and greased tin for 1 to 1¼ hours at 190°C, 375°F, Gas 5.

OLD WELSH GINGERBREAD

It will be noted that this recipe does not include ginger. This is the recipe which was used to make what was called ginger bread at some of the old Welsh fairs. A heaped teaspoonful of ground ginger can be added to this recipe if desired.

2.5 ml (½ tsp) bicarbonate of soda	50 g (2 oz) chopped candied peel
5 ml (1 tsp) cream of tartar	175 g (6 oz) black treacle,
350 g (12 oz) plain flour	which has been slightly
100 g (4 oz) butter	warmed and mixed with
175 g (6 oz) demerara sugar	150 ml (5 fl oz) of milk

Preheat the oven to 170°C, 325°F, Gas 3. Add the bicarbonate of soda and the cream of tartar to the flour and sift well into a bowl. Rub the butter into the flour, add the sugar and the peel and mix with the treacle-milk mixture. Bake in a well-greased tin for 1½ hours.

FARMHOUSE DRIPPING CAKE

350 g (12 oz) plain flour	100 g (4 oz) currants
15 ml (1 tbsp) baking powder	100 g (4 oz) sultanas
1.5 ml (¼ tsp) nutmeg	1 egg, beaten
50 g (2 oz) butter	150 ml (¼ pint) milk

175 g (6 oz) dripping   pinch of salt
175 g (6 oz) brown sugar

Preheat the oven to 190°C, 375°F, Gas 5. Sift the flour, baking powder and ground nutmeg. Rub the butter and the dripping into the flour. Stir in the sugar, the fruit and a pinch of salt. Mix the ingredients well, but lightly, as the egg with the milk are gradually added. Turn into a prepared cake tin, and bake in a moderate oven for 1½ hours.

FARMHOUSE LARD CAKE

450 g (1 lb) of ready-prepared   50 g (2 oz) lemon peel
  bread dough   50 g (2 oz) sugar
250 g (8 oz) lard   plain flour
100 g (4 oz) currants

Place the dough on a floured wooden board, and roll it out until it is about 2.5 cm (1 inch) in thickness. Spread 50 g (2 oz) of the lard on the dough, and then do the same with 50 g (2 oz) of the currants and 30 g (1 oz) of the lemon peel, then sift over it some of the sugar and a little flour. Fold the dough over, and roll it out again and spread with another 50 g (2 oz) of lard, 50 g (2 oz) of currants and 30 g (1 oz) of lemon peel, and sugar and a little flour. Repeat the rolling and larding, and adding the sugar until the dough has been rolled out 4 times.

Handle the dough lightly, and avoid pressing down heavily with the rolling pin. Cook in a well-greased tin in a moderate oven for approximately 1 hour. Cut into squares, and serve either hot or cold with butter.

ANGLESEY CAKE (1) (*TEISEN SIR FÔN*)

250 g (8 oz) butter	*2 eggs, well beaten*
350 g (12 oz) plain flour	*milk to mix*
250 g (8 oz) sugar	*a little dried fruit*
15 ml (3 tsp) baking powder	

Preheat the oven to 190°C, 375°F, Gas 5. Rub the butter into the flour. Add the sugar, baking powder, dried fruit and the eggs, and milk as necessary: the mixture ought to be fairly stiff. Divide the mixture into two greased sandwich tins. Bake for 30–40 minutes.

Cut the cakes in half and spread generously with butter. These cakes should be eaten hot.

ANGLESEY CAKE (2) (*TEISEN SIR FÔN*)

275 g (10 oz) plain flour	*15 ml (1 tbsp) of treacle*
2.5 ml (½ tsp) bicarbonate of soda	*pinch of mixed spice and ginger*
100 g (4 oz) lard or butter	*100 g (4 oz) dried fruit*
75 g (3 oz) sugar	*225 ml (7 fl oz) milk*
1 egg	*pinch of salt*

Preheat the oven to 190°C, 375°F, Gas 5. Cream the sugar and the lard or butter together. Dissolve the bicarbonate of soda in the milk. Mix the egg into the butter and sugar and add the remaining ingredients. Bake in a greased tin for approximately ¾ hour in a moderate oven.

HOT CAKE (*TEISEN BOETH*)

50 g (2 oz) butter	*2 eggs, beaten (or 1 egg*
50 g (2 oz) sugar	*mixed with a little milk)*
100 g (4 oz) plain flour	*5 ml (1 tsp) of baking powder*

Cream together the butter and the sugar. Mix together the flour and the baking powder, and add the eggs and the flour alternately. Divide the mixture into two sandwich tins and bake in a hot oven for 12–15 minutes.

Have ready some more butter already softened, and spread it as thickly as possible on the just-cooked cakes. Put the two cakes together. Sprinkle the top generously with sugar. Dried fruit can be added if wished.

EGG WHEY (*MAIDD YR IÂR*)

a thick slice of bread
1 or 2 eggs, well beaten
300 ml (½ pint) milk
a little nutmeg, ginger and
sugar

Break the bread into a saucepan. Add the eggs and the milk, then the nutmeg, the ginger and the sugar. Put on a low heat on the hob, and allow to stand until it sets; do not allow to boil.

Alternatively egg whey can be cooked in a cool oven, as for egg custard.

WELSH TEA CAKES

250 g (8 oz) flour
5 ml (1 tsp) baking powder
50 g (2 oz) butter
30 g (1 oz) sugar
1 egg
a little milk
raisins or currants
(optional)

Preheat the oven to 180°C, 350°F, Gas 5, if used. Sift together the flour and the baking powder into a bowl. Rub the butter into the flour, stir in the sugar, and mix lightly with the egg and sufficient milk to make a soft dough. Roll out, and cut into rounds with a small cutter. Raisins or currants can be added, if wished. Bake in a moderately hot oven for 20 minutes or until brown, bake as for griddle cakes.

PLANK PASTRY

100 g (4 oz) fat	jam
250 g (8 oz) flour	sugar

Rub the fat into the flour. Add water to make a firm paste. Roll out thinly and cut into two rounds, measuring with a plate. Spread one round with jam and place the other round on top. Bake on a griddle, but not too quickly. Turn over and bake on the other side. Sprinkle liberally with sugar.

WELSH CURD CAKES

600 ml (1 pint) firm, set junket	15 g (½ oz) cake crumbs
50 g (2 oz) butter	rind of 1 lemon
15 g (½ oz) sugar	5 ml (1 tsp) brandy
2 egg yolks	a pinch of salt
15 g (½ oz) currants	shortcrust pastry

Preheat the oven to 200°C, 400°F, Gas 6. Cut the junket and drain it through muslin, or a fine sieve, to remove the whey. Cream together the butter and the sugar. Add the egg yolks, the remaining ingredients and curds. Line patty tins with the pastry, and fill with the mixture. Bake in a moderately hot oven for 15 to 20 minutes.

CHEESE MUFFINS

1 egg	20 ml (4 tsp) baking
1.5 ml (¼ tsp) salt	powder
150 ml (¼ pint) milk	50 g (2 oz) grated
175 g (6 oz) plain flour	cheese

Preheat the oven to 220°C, 425°F, Gas 7. Lightly beat the egg. Add the salt and the milk. Sift together the flour and the baking powder, and then add the grated cheese. Add the liquid to the dry ingredients, beat well, forming a dough. Roll out the dough and cut into rounds, brush with beaten egg, and bake on a greased baking sheet in a hot oven for 10 minutes.

Split and serve spread with butter. Can be eaten hot or cold.

CAERPHILLY SCONES (*SGONAU CAERFFILI*)

350 g (12 oz) flour	150 g (5 oz) Caerphilly
1.5 ml (¼ tsp) salt	cheese
15 ml (3 tsp) baking powder	300 ml (½ pint) milk
40 g (1½ oz) butter	pepper to taste

Preheat the oven to 220°C, 425°F, Gas 7. Sift together the flour, salt and the baking powder. Rub in the butter. Grate the cheese with a fine grater, and add to the flour with the pepper. Mix all the ingredients well, and then add enough milk to form a soft dough. Roll out to about 2.5 cm (½ in) in thickness, and cut into rounds. Place on a baking sheet, greased with butter. Bake in a hot oven for 15 to 20 minutes.

Serve hot, spread with butter.

TINKER'S APPLE CAKE (*DINCA FALA*)

150 g (5 oz) butter	450 g (1 lb) cooking
275 g (10 oz) self-raising	apples, peeled and
flour	cut into small pieces
150 g (5 oz) demerara sugar	sufficient milk to mix

Preheat the oven to 200°C, 400°F, Gas 6. Rub the butter

into the flour. Add the sugar and the apples. Add enough milk to make a fairly stiff mixture. Put the mixture into a greased tin and bake for ½ hour until golden brown.

RICE PUDDING (*PWDIN REIS*)

50 g (2 oz) pudding rice	2.5 ml (½ tsp) grated
30 g (1 oz) butter	nutmeg
50 g (2 oz) demerara sugar	1 or 2 separated eggs
600 ml (1 pint) milk	pinch of salt

Simmer the rice in 300 ml (½ pint) water until the grain is swollen. Add the butter, the sugar, the milk, a pinch of salt and the nutmeg. Simmer gently for approximately 2 hours. Remove from the heat, and beat in the egg yolks. Beat the egg whites until stiff, and fold into the pudding just before serving.

SNOWDON PUDDING (*PWDIN ERYRI*)

250 g (8 oz) suet	250 g (8 oz) fresh bread
40 g (1½ oz) ground rice	crumbs
175 g (6 oz) lemon	175 g (6 oz) brown
marmalade	sugar
pinch of salt	grated rind of 2 lemons
100 g (4 oz) raisins	6 eggs

Mix together all the dry ingredients and the marmalade, but reserve some of the raisins. Beat the eggs thoroughly, and add to the mixture. Grease a basin, and spread the reserved raisins over the inside, and pour in the mixture. Cover tightly and boil for 1½ hours, remembering to top up the water as it boils down.

Serve with white sauce.

WATKIN WYNNE PUDDING

375 g (3 oz) fresh bread-crumbs	3 eggs
	a pinch of salt
250 g (8 oz) chopped suet	the juice and grated
75 g (3 oz) sugar	rind of 2 lemons

Sauce

butter	grated lemon peel
brown sugar	a glass of sherry or
grated nutmeg	Madeira wine

Mix together all the ingredients well and put into a well-greased basin. Cover and boil for 3 hours until cooked.

For the sauce, melt butter with brown sugar, add the grated lemon peel and nutmeg, with a glass of sherry or Madeira. It is important that the sauce is hot, but it should not be allowed to boil. Serve immediately.

CHRISTMAS CAKE (*TEISIN 'DOLIG*)

This is an old recipe from Cardigan.

15 g (½ oz) yeast	100 g (4 oz) almonds
675 g (1½ lb) plain flour	½ nutmeg, grated
250 g (8 oz) butter	mixed spice
450 g (1 lb) caster sugar	juice of half an orange
100 g (4 oz) mixed peel	and half a lemon
250 g (8 oz) sultanas	home brew or 1 bottle
250 g (8 oz) currants	of pale ale
250 g (8 oz) raisins	

Preheat the oven for 190°C, 375°F, Gas 5. Rub the yeast into the flour. Rub in the butter, sugar, fruit, nuts and spices. Add the fruit juices, and the home brew or pale ale. Use only enough of the ale to moisten the mixture:

it is important to ensure that the mixture does not become too soft. Put the mixture into a lined cake tin. Cook in a moderately hot oven for 3 hours.

WELSH FRUIT TART

shortcrust pastry (following sugar
recipe on p. 62) bicarbonate of soda
any fruit in season or
bottled fruit

Preheat the oven to 200°C, 400°F, Gas 6. Grease a deep plate or pie-dish. Divide the pastry into two portions. Roll out thinly, and line the plate and trim the edges. Partly cook the fruit. Fill the plate with the fruit, and sweeten with sugar. Sprinkle a little bicarbonate of soda around the edges of the fruit to prevent the juice from escaping. Cover with the remaining pastry. Pinch together the edges after wetting with water, then cut holes in the top to allow the steam to escape. Bake in a hot oven for 20 minutes.

PLUM TART (*TARTEN EIRIN*)

shortcrust pastry (following a pinch of mixed spice
recipe on p. 62) 2.5 ml (½ tsp) cinnamon
100 g (4 oz) fat 15 g (½ oz) sugar
250 g (8 oz) plain flour

The filling

450 g (1 lb) plums, cut in 100 g (4 oz) sugar
half and stoned A little water
4 small apples, sliced

Preheat the oven to 200°C, 400°F, Gas 6. Rub the fat into

the flour and the spices, until it resembles fine bread-crumbs. Stir in the sugar and add enough water to make a firm paste. Divide the pastry into two portions, and roll out. Line a greased plate or shallow pie-dish with half the pastry. Reserve the remainder for the pie crust.

Fill the lined plate or dish with the fruit. Cover with sugar and add a little water. Cover with the remaining pastry.

Bake for 20 minutes, then lower to 180°C, 350°F, Gas 4 for 25 minutes.

GRIDDLE CAKE (6) (*TEISEN LAP*)

A griddle cake, made with a fairly wet mixture. Originally this cake was cooked in a Dutch oven before an open fire, but the result is as good if it is baked on a well-greased baking tin.

450 g (1 lb) plain flour	*50 g (2 oz) currants*
5 ml (1 tsp) baking powder	*50 g (2 oz) sultanas*
a pinch of salt	*3 eggs*
a little grated nutmeg	*300 ml (½ pint) milk*
100 g (4 oz) butter	*(sour milk is ideal)*
100 g (4 oz) sugar	

Preheat the oven to 190°C, 375°F, Gas 5. Sieve the flour with the baking powder, salt and nutmeg. Rub in the butter lightly. Add the sugar and the fruit. Beat the eggs thoroughly and add to the mixture. Gradually add the milk, mixing all the time with a wooden spoon. The mixture should be soft enough to drop from the spoon. Spread out thinly in the prepared tin. Bake for 35 to 45 minutes in a moderately hot oven.

Preserves

GOOSEBERRY MINT JELLY

1.8 kg (4 lb) green
   gooseberries
sugar

approximately six stalks
   fresh mint

Wipe the gooseberries and put them into a preserving pan. Cover with cold water and cook until the fruit is soft. Strain carefully. Measure the strained juice, and for each 600 ml (1 pint) juice, weigh 450 g (1 lb) sugar, which should be warmed. Return the liquid to the preserving pan, and add the mint, which should be tied in a bundle. Heat gently, stirring until the sugar is dissolved. Boil, without stirring, until it reaches setting point (about 104°C, 220°F). Remove the mint, allow to cool, and pour into heated glass jars and seal immediately.

BLACKCURRANT JAM

1.8 kg (4 lb) blackcurrants

2.75 kg (6 lb) sugar,
   warmed

Put the fruit and 1.4 litres (2½ pints) cold water into a preserving pan and bring to the boil. Lower the heat, and simmer gently until the fruit is soft. Add the sugar, and stir until it dissolves. Boil again for approximately 8 to 10 minutes. Allow the jam to cool before pouring into heated jars, and seal immediately

BLACKBERRY JAM

2.75 kg (6 lb) blackberries   2.75 kg (6 lb) sugar

Put the fruit into a large saucepan, add 15 ml (1 tbsp) cold water, and place in a warm place for several hours, remembering to stir the fruit from time to time. Gently heat, and when just on the point of boiling, add the sugar and boil quickly for only 3 minutes. Pour the jam into warm jars when it has cooled.

RHUBARB JAM

2.75 kg (6 lb) rhubarb   juice and rind of 2 lemons
finely chopped   6 cloves and half a
2.75 (6 lb) sugar, warmed   nutmeg tied in a muslin
50 g (2 oz) chopped almonds   bag

Cut the rhubarb into small pieces, then put in a large saucepan and leave to stand in a warm place for several hours. When the juice is seen to seep from the fruit, add the sugar together with the almonds and the lemon juice and rind. Boil all together until the jam thickens, about 15 minutes. Gently skim off any scum from the surface of the jam. Then add the cloves and the nutmeg tied in the muslin bag, and allow the jam to stand until it cools. Remove the muslin bag, and put the jam into warm jars, and cover.

Drinks

It is worth remembering that any fermented drink made with yeast will have an alcoholic content.

OLD MEAD (*MEDD*)

Mead was traditionally made in the autumn so that it would mature in time for the Christmas festivities.

for each 4.5 litres (1 gallon) of wine:
1.8 kg (4 lb) honey   *15 g (½ oz) hops*
30 g (1 oz) ginger   *toasted bread*
a good pinch of allspice

Boil the honey and the water for 1 hour, and then skim. Add the ginger and the allspice and boil for another 10 minutes. Strain it, and add the hops on a piece of toasted bread and leave it for 2 days. Skim it off, and put the liquor into a suitable jar, if possible a stone jar. When the mead has finished fermenting, bung down tightly.

Alternatively the mead can be put into smaller stone bottles. Allow to stand several weeks before drinking.

OAK LEAF WINE (*GWIN DAIL Y DDERWEN*)
For each 4.5 litres (1 gallon) of wine:

about 2.25 litres (4 pints) loosely packed clean brown withered oak leaves, which should be picked from the tree on a dry day

a piece of root ginger
1.8 kg (4 lb) granulated sugar
450 g (1 lb) raisins or sultanas
15 g (½ oz) yeast

Place the leaves in a bowl, ideally one made of earthenware, and pour on sufficient boiling water to cover them. Allow the leaves to infuse for 4 to 5 days, then strain. Boil the strained liquid, adding the ginger and the sugar. After the liquid has boiled for 20 minutes, allow it to cool until lukewarm, and return it to the original vessel. Add the raisins or sultanas and the yeast. Cover well and allow to ferment for 16 days in a warm place. Strain and bottle. The wine should be ready to drink in 3 months, but does improve as it matures.

PRIMROSE WINE (*GWIN BRIALLU*)

2.25 litres (4 pints) of primrose petals
450 g (1 lb) chopped raisins

1.4 kg (3 lb) sugar
450 g (1 lb) wheat
30 g (1 oz) yeast

Steep the primrose petals in 4.5 litres (1 gallon) cold water for 8 days, then squeeze them out. Put the raisins, the sugar and the wheat into the liquid and stir until the sugar has dissolved. Sprinkle the yeast on top of the liquid, and leave to ferment for 28 days. Skim, strain and bottle.

RHUBARB WINE (*GWIN RHIWBOB*)

1.8 kg (4 lbs) rhubarb   *50 g (2 oz) ginger*
1.62 kg (3½ lb) sugar   *30 g (1 oz) cloves*

Cut the rhubarb into small pieces, but do not peel. Place in a pan with 4.5 litres (1 gallon) water. Let it stand for 4 days, stirring occasionally, until the fruit softens. Strain and add the sugar, and stir until it is dissolved. Boil the ginger and the cloves in some of the liquid, and then leave it to go cold, before pouring it back into the rest of the liquid. Stir, skimming it as necessary every day, until the first vigorous fermentation ceases: about 7 days. Bottle it, but do not cork tightly until all fermentation has ceased.

NETTLE AND BURDOCK DRINK

2 litres (4 pints) of young   *900 g (2 lb) sugar*
* nettles*   *1 lemon*
50 g (2 oz) burdock leaves   *50 g (2 oz) yeast*
50 g (2 oz) hops   *toasted bread*

Boil the nettles, the burdock and the hops gently in 4.5 litres (1 gallon) water for 30 minutes. Strain, and add the sugar and the lemon, cut into small pieces. Leave until the liquid is lukewarm. Put the yeast, spread on a slice of toasted bread, on top of the liquid. Leave for 12 hours. Strain, and bottle and make airtight. Can be drunk after 12 hours.

DAISY WINE (*GWIN LLYGAD Y DYDD*)

4.5 litres (1 gallon) of small   *1.1 kg(2½ lb) brown sugar*
* field daisy flowers*   *100 g (4 oz) chopped*
2 lemons, sliced   * raisins*
2 oranges, sliced   *30 g (1 oz) yeast*

Put the daisy heads in a bowl and cover with 4.5 litres (1 gallon) boiling water. Allow to stand until the next day. Squeeze the daisies out. Boil the liquid with the lemons and the oranges and the sugar for 20 minutes. Allow to cool until lukewarm. Add the raisins and stir in the yeast, which should be dissolved first with a little warm water. Leave to ferment for 2 weeks. Then skim, strain and bottle.

DANDELION WINE (*GWIN DANT Y LLEW*)

3 kg (6 lb) of dandelion flowers, picked on a dry, sunny day	2 lemons
	1 orange
	15 g (½ oz) yeast
1.4 kg (3 lb) sugar	toasted bread

Pour 4.5 litres (1 gallon) boiling water over the dandelion flowers. Cover with a thick cloth, and allow to stand for 24 hours, stirring both night and morning. Strain, and to every 4.5 litres (1 gallon) of liquid add 1.4 kg (3 lb) of sugar, the juice and rind of the lemons and the orange, but omitting the white pith. Boil for 30 minutes. Allow it to cool, and then add 15 g (½ oz) yeast spread on a piece of toasted bread. Float the toast on the surface of the liquid. Allow the liquid to ferment for 3 to 4 days. Strain, and pour the wine into bottles, corking loosely at first, and then tightening them when the fermentation process is completed.

APPLE WINE (*GWIN AFALAU*)

1.8 kg (4 lb) of apples	piece of bruised ginger
sugar	juice of 2 lemons
a few cloves	

Crush the apples, and pour over 4.5 litres (1 gallon) boiling water, cover with a cloth and leave for 14 days, squeezing each day. Strain, add the cloves and the ginger, and add 250 g (8 oz) sugar for each 600 ml (1 pint) of liquid. Add the lemon juice, stir well until the sugar has dissolved. Leave to stand until a scum forms on the surface of the liquid. Skim, pour into bottles, and cork tightly.

GINGER BEER (*CWRW SINSIR*)

Half-fill a 6 litre (10 pint) saucepan with nettles and dandelions in equal quantities, together with 2 sticks of rhubarb and 4 sticks of pounded ginger. Fill the saucepan with cold water. Boil for 15 minutes, with a handful of currant leaves. Strain and add 450 g (1 lb) of sugar to the liquid. Stir, and add 4.5 litres (1 gallon) of cold water. When the liquid is lukewarm, mix 30 g (1 oz) yeast in a cup of the liquid, and add to the remainder. Leave in a warm place overnight. The next day skim off the yeast and bottle the liquid. Do not cork too tightly at first.

DAMSON PORT (*GWIN EIRIN DUON*)

1.8 kg (4 lb) damson plums   1.8 kg (4 lb) sugar

Pour 4.5 litres (1 gallon) boiling water over the plums, and leave to infuse for 10 days, stirring and squeezing the fruit each day. Then run through a jelly bag, and then strain twice without squeezing. Add the sugar to the liquid and stir until it has completely dissolved. Stir in a teacupful of boiling water and leave to ferment for 14 days. Skim and bottle, corking very loosely at first.

NETTLE SYRUP (*GWIN DANADL POETHION*)

It is said that this syrup has blood-purifying qualities.
Gather the tops of young nettles and wash well. To
every 450 g (1 lb) of nettles add 1 litre (2 pints) of cold
water. Boil for 1 hour. Strain, adding to every 600 ml (1
pint) of the infusion 450 g (1 lb) of sugar. Boil for 30
minutes, and bottle when cold.

Miscellaneous

WELSH RAREBIT (*CAWS WEDI'I BOBI*)

100 g (4 oz) grated cheese	*beer (optional)*
45 ml (3 tbsp) milk	*toasted bread*
30 g (1 oz) butter	*salt and pepper*
mustard (optional)	

Place the cheese and the milk in a saucepan and melt gently. Add the seasoning, mustard (if required) and the butter, and stir gently. When the sauce is very hot, pour over the slice of toast, and brown under a grill. A little beer can be added to the sauce if wished.

TOCYN Y CARDI
An accompaniment to bacon.

15 ml (1 tbsp) rolled oats	*a pinch of salt*
15 ml (1 tbsp) plain flour	*30 ml (2 tbsp) milk*
15 ml (1 tbsp) baking powder	*bacon fat*

Mix all the dry ingredients together. Make the mixture into small cakes, and fry in bacon fat.
   Serve with fried bacon.

OATMEAL TROLLIES

250 g (8 oz) fine oatmeal	*50 g (2 oz) suet*
50 g (2 oz) self-raising flour	*50 g (2 oz) currants*
a pinch of salt	*milk or water to mix*

Mix all the dry ingredients together. Make a firm dough with either milk or water. Make into trollies, which should be about the size of an egg. Boil in any soup or *cawl* for approximately 45 minutes. Trollies can be served with boiled bacon.

WELSH BREAD (*BARA CYMREIG*)

30 g (1 oz) yeast	900 g (2 lb) white flour
30 g (1 oz) sugar	900 g (2 lb) brown flour
30 g (1 oz) butter	15 g (½ oz) salt

Mix together the yeast and the sugar. Add the butter to the warm water. Sift the flours with the salt into a large mixing bowl. Add the yeast, sugar and 900 ml (1½ pints) warm water to the flour. Mix into a dough, and knead well. Half-fill greased loaf tins with the dough, and leave to rise in a warm place. Bake in a hot oven (200°C, 400°F, Gas 6) for 35 to 45 minutes.

TREACLE TOFFEE (*TAFFI TRIOG*)
This toffee used to be made at Christmas.

450 g (1 lb) demerara sugar	50 g (2 oz) butter
250 ml (8 fl oz) water	30 ml (2 tbsp) treacle
a drop or two of vinegar	nuts (optional)

Put all the ingredients into a saucepan and boil very quickly for 2 minutes. Pour into a greased oblong tin. When cold cut into small squares.

HOT SAUCE
A very old recipe. This sauce will keep for years, so it is said.

60 ml (4 tbsp) mustard powder	60 ml (4 tbsp) spices
60 ml (4 tbsp) flour or corn-flour	30 ml (2 tbsp) salt
1 litre (1¾ pints) vinegar	a pinch of cayenne pepper
30 ml (2 tbsp) black treacle	6 lumps sugar

Mix the mustard and the flour or cornflour with a little of the vinegar. Add all the other ingredients to the remaining vinegar, and boil for 10 minutes. Add the flour and mustard mixture and boil for another 5 or 10 minutes. Strain and allow to cool. Skim and bottle.

TREACLE POSSET

A medicinal drink. This is an excellent drink for colds, and should be taken in bed.

300 ml (½ pint) buttermilk or milk	30 ml (2 tbsp) of treacle

Put the buttermilk or milk into a saucepan, and bring it to the boil. Add the treacle and bring to the boil again. Stand for a few minutes in a warm place. Drain and serve hot.

FLUMMERY (*LLYMRU*)

4 tbsp oatmeal	a little ginger
a little sugar	

Add the oatmeal to 1 litre (2 pints) cold water, and allow it to stand for 6 days. Pour off the water clearly. Strain through a sieve, and boil it until it has thickened, while stirring it all the time. Flavour with a little ginger and sugar.

OATCAKE BROSE (*BRYWAS*)

Half-fill a bowl with small pieces of bread. Pour over boiling water until the bowl is almost full. Crush about half an oatcake with a rolling pin, and add to the bread and water mixture. Add a little salt and pepper to flavour and place in a dish. Melt 30 g (1 oz) or a little more of suet or beef dripping in a pan. Pour the melted fat over the other ingredients. Sprinkle some more oatcakes on the top. Let it stand for several minutes.

Potatoes may be used instead of bread.

SHORTCRUST PASTRY

250 g (8 oz) plain flour   50 g (2 oz) butter
50 g (2 oz) lard   a pinch of salt

Sift the flour and the salt into a bowl. Rub in the lard and the butter until the mixture resembles fine bread-crumbs. Add cold water slowly to form a fairly firm paste. Turn on to a floured board and knead lightly. Roll out and use as required.

Index